Copyrighted material

First edition August 10, 2018

ISBN: 978-0-994 -7055-4-9

Independently published

Republic of South Africa

Product details:

Item Weight: 5.9 ounces

Pack back: 236 pages

Product Dimension: 6 x 0.46 x 9 inches

Publisher: Adebisi Dawodu SA PTY LTD

Languages: English

Designer: Adebisi Dawodu

Layout: Adebisi Dawodu

Website: aste-sa.buiness.site

Living beyond the limit:

"Limitations are visible phenomena that appear or happen in the human world or endeavours.

Contents:

Living beyond the limit:

About the Author:

Adebisi Dawodu is known as Shalom as an Author, was born in Lagos Nigeria. Where he undergo His Primary and Secondary School education, before enrolled at Mountain of Fire Miracle Ministries (MFM), for Diploma in the school of prayer (SOP) Theology at Matthew Street Ojuelebga Lagos Nigeria.

After the completion of His Theological program? He was posted to Mountain of Fire Miracle Ministries (MFM) Ibadan, Oyo State, Nigeria. Where he did His ministerial industrial training IT, concluding His ministerial industrial training? He got a ministerial appointment at Christ the Redeemers Ministries (CRM) situated at Ogun State, Nigeria. Before, the ministerial appointment? He studied, Certificate in Computer application with the computer training school of the ministries, before He started His ministerial appointment with the ministries.

In the course of His ministerial appointment? He enrolled at Rufus Giwa Polytechnic Owo. Where He studied Diploma in Business Studies, in their satellite campus situated at Agege Lagos State, Nigeria. He was given leave in 2005, where he spent His two weeks leave at Seychelles Island. Returning from His vacation? He discoursed His intention of studying abroad with His Coordinator, of studying in South Africa.

Arriving in South Africa in 2005 November 26? He enrolled at Intec College, where he did a module in Web page design. He concluded His College with Edusa SA, where he completed a Diploma in Graphic design and multimedia in 2009. Concluding his college qualification? He enrolled with Redeemed Christian Bible College South Africa (RCBC SA) the Theology School of the ministries, where He worked with, in Nigeria. Where He studied Certificate in Theology in 2010. In the course of the Theological program with RCBC SA? He was appointed from His provincial Headquarters, Recharge Centre Ogun Province 4, Ogun State Nigeria.

The ministry arms of the ministries where he worked with, in Nigeria.

That came to plant a church in South-gate Johannesburg South Africa in 2010.

He resigned with the ministries, both the Church arms and the ministries in 2012. The Author (Adebisi Dawodu, known as Shalom as an Author) began His own ministries, which began with psychologist and motivation, Author and along the line? He included Prison ministries that commence in South Africa Prisons in 2019.

In His ministerial career? Both in ministries and other professions! He continued with His studies. Studying with the University of South Africa (UNISA) where He is currently studying Archive and Records managements.

Adebisi Dawodu is known as Shalom as an Author, has gained experience in ministries since His ministerial industrial training to date and has published sixteen books.

Dedication: I dedicated this book! Living beyond the limit to God Almighty. I gave Him the glory for making it possible for this dream to become a reality.

ISBN Number: 978-0-994 -7055-4-9

Second edition: 2022

Introduction: Living beyond the limit is faith-building, deliverance, spiritual growth, and inspiration! Which can be used as a daily devotional and prayer into the will of God for one purpose in life.

From the first series, lots of mechanisms and faith-building that can enable and guide one way and destiny in achieving its purpose are substantially looked into.

Also, prayer and Bible verses that can enable one path to achieve its deliverances and live great in life also included in the series.

As it's known as a faith-building and deliverances! Impaction that will enhance the faith-building and deliverances in one victory path is also included from the beginning of the series to the ending of the series.

For one to achieve the result of the series? From the beginning to the ending! One needs to engage with the inspirational, prayer, and Bible verses that are in the series in order to achieve substantial results in deliverances and faith-building.

In other words, it can also be used as a morning devotional, and when challenges and difficulties are making one life horrible experiences and when it seemed one is not living up to his or her projected vision, goals, and dream that one has set before the beginning of the year and with what one his experiencing with at the moment.

Such one may be in need of spirit-led inspiration and daily living materials to achieve his or her deliverance and victory over what has been making one life a mountain to climb. Also, it makes one grow in Bible studies, and having an understanding of the scripture through the Holy Spirit! And how to apply it in one daily endeavour, and achieve great success of the limit and limitations of life.

‘’Living beyond the limit.

Living, beyond the limit! 1

(Habakkuk 3:17 – 18 NKJV). Although the fig tree shall not blossom, neither shall fruit be in the vines, the labour of the olive shall fail, and the fields shall yield no meat, the flock shall be cut off from the fold, and there shall be no herd in the stalls. Vs18. Yet I will rejoice in the Lord, I will joy in the God of my salvation.

Limitations are visible phenomena that appear or happen in the human world or endeavours, and these visible elements occur in stages. Which determine the productivities, progress, and achievement of an individual towards target goals, dreams, or vision and affect one destiny in an unpleasant circumstance.

In other words, the operation of limit or limitation in the lives of its victims? Can be resulted in not being able to progress in life, starting a project and not being able to accomplish it at the appropriate timing.

Also, it can be resulted in to delay in one achievement and success in life. A limitation is a major phenomenon or cause of not being able to excel or fulfilling one goal and purpose in life.

''Breaking the bound.

Prophet Habakkuk understood or has, a deep knowledge of what is going on in his surroundings, he knew, that there is a limit or limitation standing between him and his goodness! But he decides to live beyond the limit, and he uses the weapons of deliverances.

''Praises and prayer are weaponry of liberation.

There will always be some stages or a point in our lives we may experience limits or limitations! But our response to it will determine if we will overcome it or live beyond it. In other words, right responses such as praise and prayer are the earnest important weapon that can give you and me a lasting victory, are you experiencing such in your life?

Prayer: I encourage you to use praise and prayer. And testimony will be your portion in the name of Jesus. Amen.

LIVING, BEYOND THE LIMIT! 2

"limitations are visible phenomenon that appears or happens in the human world or endeavour, and these visible elements occur in stages.

(Zechariah 4:7 NKJV). Who are thou, o great mountain? Before Zerubbabel, thou shalt become a plain, and he shall bring forth the headstone thereof with shouting's, crying, Grace, grace unto it.

"The mystery of limit or limitation? Are unimaginable occurrences that try to

influence our lives, purpose, goals, or destiny.

Which its occurrences have to be a fathom for us not to understand and handle in our own strength or abilities. But little did we know that? The operation of limit or limitation in our lives? Are activities designed or orchestrated by the enemies or the devil to hinder us in our goals or vision in life?

In other words, know-how? Well structured! Design or program activities of limit or limitation maybe? It can be handled or solved by using the right response.

''Right response to limit or limitation.

At every challenge circumstance or difficulty that may be facing one-in-life? There is always a solution to overcoming the strange circumstances that have been making life unliveable and success unachievable for us.

In other words, living righteously and obeying every commandment of God, for one in life! Is one of the right responses to overcoming limits or limitations in one life.

"Zerubbabel acknowledged the right response.

Nothing could have happened in the life of Zerubbabel. If he's not right position or right standing in God. Sin is the total element that destroys the relationship between God and men. And it has been a barrier to not receiving from God and not being fruitful in life.

Also, for us to tell the limit or limitation where they belong? We need to live a sin-free life and be obedient imitators of Christ.

Prayer: you will live beyond every limit and limitation of life in this year and beyond in the name of Jesus. Amen.

LIVING, BEYOND THE LIMIT! 3

'The mystery of limit or limitation? Are unimaginable occurrences that try to influence our lives, purpose, goals, or destiny. Which occurrences have to be been a fathom for us not to understand and handle in our own strength or abilities.

(Daniel 11:32b). *But the people that do know their God shall be strong and do exploits.*

"**The first fundamental principle or first things first?** In living beyond the limit and limitation! Is to be in the family of God and to imitate Christ.

Living beyond the limit or limitation? Is not acquired by self-sufficiency, nor is it achieved by individual skills, competencies, or abilities. In other words, to live beyond the limit or limitation? Is rooted in having a piece of full knowledge of God and being an imitator of Christ.

Also, Daniel, Shadrach, Meshach, and Abednego could have bowed down to the demon in Babylon! If they did not have, have! The first fundamental principle and to imitate Christ.

Daniel 3:14. And Nebuchadnezzar said to them, "Is it true, Shadrach, Meshach, and

Abednego, that you do not serve my gods or worship the image of gold I have set up?

''*Stand your ground.*

Everyone that lives beyond the limit or limitation? They stood on their ground! They did not allow unbelief to droves them from one stage to another.

They stood on their faith in God! And steadfast in their trust in the living Lord, who is able to make them live beyond challenges or circumstances that may be befalling them in life.

In other words, Shadrach, Meshach, and Abednego are good examples of those that stood on their faith in God that did not allow limits or limitations to droves them all around. They live beyond their limit and limitation.

Daniel 3:25 – 26. He said, "Look! I see four men walking around in the fire, unbound and unharmed, and the fourth looks like a son of the gods."[26] Nebuchadnezzar then approached the opening of the blazing furnace and shouted, "Shadrach, Meshach, and Abednego, servants of the Most-High God, come out! Come here!" So Shadrach, Meshach, and Abednego came out of the fire,

''Let limit and limitation obey you.

Having the right knowledge of God and being steadfast in faith? Will bring circumstances or challenges to subjection and defeating every enemy that says! You will not live beyond limits or limitations this year.

Prayer: limit and limitation will all bow down to Christ in you. In Jesus's name. Amen.

LIVING, BEYOND THE LIMIT! 4

'The first fundamental principles or first things first? In living beyond the limit or limitation! Is, to be in the family of God, and to imitate Christ.

(1 Chronicle 4:9 NKJV). And Jabez was more honourable than his brethren, and his mother called his name Jabez, saying Because I bare him with sorrow.

"**You may have gotten the prestige!** And more respected among colleagues and in the societies but still lives in limits and limitations.

At known, how! Humanly endowment? That anyone may possess or achieve. That does not mean such one! Is, living beyond the limit or limitation.

In other words, limit or limitation? Are, the circumstance or challenges that occurred or appeared in one life, in stages or could be found in one foundation.

Also, limit or limitation? Are resistances, that limit the progress of an individual, not to progress to the higher level of success, and also, which is capable of hindering one destiny not to achieve it! Divine purpose, that has been ordained before one was giving-birth-to. And such can be linked to foundational problems or issues.

''Breaking the yoke of limit and limitation off you.

Jabez acknowledged or had an understanding of that! For him to move forward in life or to achieve his purpose in his lifetime? He has to break the yoke of limits and limitations that have been resisting him not to live in the atmosphere of great achievers. In other words, he acknowledged, that! He cannot do that! Or achieved it, by himself.

1 Chronicle 4:10. And Jabez called on the God of Israel, saying, Oh that thou wouldest bless me indeed, and enlarge my coast, and that thine hand might be with me, and that thou wouldest keep me from evil, that it may not grieve me! And God granted him that which he requested.

''*Jesus, is the yoke breaker*.

Whatever, that may seem like a mountain to climb, if there is any. Or challenges? Which such is beyond, your reasons! Take it, to Jesus. Is the yoke breaker. In other words, you cannot defeat or overcome limits or limitations. By just seating, and doing nothing! With regard to it.

You will defeat it, by living righteously, studying the scripture, and taking it to God.

Prayer: the living lord, will grant your request in Jesus's name. Amen.

LIVING, BEYOND THE LIMIT! 5

"You may have gotten the prestige! And more respected among colleagues and in the societies but still lives in limits and limitations.

(Proverbs 1:5 NKJV). A wise man will hear and will increase learning, and a man of understanding shall attain unto wise counsels.

"W**isdom is profitable to direct** and yield to divine instruction? Will guide us in every stage of our lives! And making us be victories in life.

Much of sighting strange occurrences that have been making life unliveable, having a sleepless night, or challenging your faith in God? Can be handled! By, yielding to divine instruction and by, the knowledge you have acquired in God's words, to-leads you to the path of lasting victories.

In other words, the journey of living! Beyond the limit and limitations in life? Can be, simply be! In obedient to God's commandments and instructions given from his words, and applying wisdom! Which is the application of knowledge.

"*Applying wisdom, application of knowledge.*

To every situation in human lives? There is always a solution. Whatever! That is, without a solution? And is present in a human's habitat? Just know that such does not exist in the same world, that I and you! Are living.

In other words, in God's master plan? Everything God has created; he has a solution for each of them. To solve and handle.

"***Creation master plan***.

Talking of creation? We are simply referring to God. Jehovah El-Elohim, God that creates.

Genesis 1:11. And God said, Let the earth bring forth grass, the herb yielding seed, and the fruit tree yielding fruit after his kind, whose seed is in itself upon the earth, and it was so.

Also, when talking about knowledge! We are simply referring to God. Jehovah El-Deah. The God of knowledge.

Proverbs 1:7. The fear of the Lord is the beginning of knowledge, but fools despise wisdom and instruction.

We can use knowledge and obedience to tell limits and limitations! Where they belong, and lasting victories will be achieved by you.

Prayer: the grace to make proper use of knowledge and obedience, will be given to you. And you will live beyond your limit and limitation in Jesus's name. Amen.

LIVING, BEYOND THE LIMIT! 6

''Wisdom! Is profitable to direct. And yielding to divine instruction? Will guide us in every stage of our lives! And making us, be victories in life.

(Esther 2:15 NKJV). Now when the turn of Esther, the daughter of Abihail the uncle of Mordecai, who had taken her for his daughter, was come to go into the king, she required nothing but what Hegai the king's chamberlain, the keeper of the woman, appointed. And Esther obtained favour in the sight of all them that looked upon her.

"**In the race of victories and success in life**, there are many that participate, but few are the chosen.

The chosen are not more, better than the many, either are they more profane or, skilful! But, there is something. What differentiates them, between them! And the many.

In other words, after a race, there is always a crown. The crown is the symbol of accomplishment and achievement in participating in a race.

Also, without a race! It will be difficult to find a participant because the participant is the recipient of the crown! That's participating in a race.

''*What, that differentiates between the many and the few.*

It has been noticed in human endeavours or is surrounding, that! Achievements for some? It has always been a challenging phenomenon, while to others? It had always been an easy ride! In achieving their aim in life.

Esther was favoured or honoured in the palace of Shushan, not because she was more profane or skilful than other maidens in the palace. She acted differently! She follows what Hegai the king's chamberlain, the keeper of the women, appointed. And that makes her the few among the many.

''*The few among the many.*

In every many, in a race? There are always a few achievers' that run a race. Living beyond, the limit or limitation in life at times? Can be achieved by yielding to what has been divinely appointed by God.

Not what we see, as best to choose or yield to. In other words, yielding to divine instruction or what that has been divinely appointed by God? Will always make one live beyond the limit and limitations in life.

Prayer: the grace to follow the leading of God, and overcome every challenging phenomenon! Will be giving you in Jesus's name. Amen.

LIVING, BEYOND THE LIMIT! 7

"In the race of victories and success in life, there are many that participate, but few are the chosen.

(Matthew 5:6 NKJV). Blessed are they which do hunger and thirst after righteousness, for they shall be filled.

"**Every candidate of greatness** and achievers! Always displays the goodness of God among others and in their endeavours.

To be great! And live beyond all limits and limitations in life? Are the treasure of living rightly and thirsting after the things of God.

There are godly candidates! That live in greatness and being an achiever, and living beyond all limits and limitations. Also, there are! The ungodly candidate that doesn't live beyond limits and limitations.

In other words, every diligence to the obedience of God and thirsting after his righteousness! Are the divine stages or platforms of qualifying to the abundance of God and living blessed in life.

No matter the strength of your enemies or your haters! Because you are on the platform of God, you will always defeat them and be an overcomer in life.

''*Godly candidate*.

Are candidate which live by the instruction of God, and by his obedience! They are being led to every endeavour of their life through the instructions of God. Also, they love righteousness and they enjoy fellowship with their maker.

In other words, they are called blessed, by their maker! Because, they imitate him, and live by his commandments. Who can curse the blessed of the Lord? Nobody. I say to you today! You are blessed by the Lord.

"*Ungodly candidate*.

Are easy to identify and they always are a target of all challenges of their enemies. Also, due to their ungodliness? Living, beyond the limit and limitations, has always been a mountainous challenge for them to achieve in life.

Are you a godly candidate or an ungodly candidate? Note! Godly candidates are the candidate that lives beyond, all limit and limitations in life.

Prayer: I see you living, beyond the limit and limitations of life! And you will achieve in Jesus's name. Amen.

LIVING, BEYOND THE LIMIT! 8

"Every candidate of greatness, and an achiever! Always displays the goodness of God among others and in their endeavours.

(Deuteronomy 20:4). For the Lord, your God is he that goeth with you, to fight for you against your enemies, to save you.

"**The battles of our victories and living abundantly against all strange occurrences**! Are not carnal but are mighty in pulling down every stronghold to the obedience of God.

Our victories lie in God, not with our strength, either our abilities in gaining grounds and giving us! A lasting victory. In other words, the mystery of limits and limitations and the strange occurrences? That we may be experiencing! Maybe, without our consent, but visibly they are appearing and limiting our position in God.

Yielding to the tone or the ideology of it will always keep us below achieving and living abundantly in life. Also, continuous focus on God and living rightly! Enables us to have a divine edge against all our difficulties.

"*Divine edge*.

The first thing first or first principles of having an access to the divine edge in God against all strange occurrences and difficulties in life? Is to be rooted in God and live by the instruction given from the word of God.

Meanwhile, every achiever in God, or those that live beyond the limit and limitations of life? Are those that abide by the instructions of God and live by his obedience.

"Giving in! To his instructions.

In the record of God, he has not lost any battles! His master in victories. Whosoever may be instructing you, or telling you? How, to live in victory and be successful in life? There is a need to check his or her biography! What battles has he or she ever won, and what is their background?

If the record retrieves are below substantial results? There is no need of yielding to such instructions. God! Is the only reliable source of all abundance and who will help you and me to be overcome in life.

Prayer: I pray in his knowledge into your life! And your testimony will abide in Jesus's name. Amen.

LIVING, BEYOND THE LIMIT! 9

"The battles of our victories, and living abundantly against all strange occurrences! Are not carnal, but are mighty in pulling down, every stronghold to the obedience of God.

(Proverbs 4:2). For I give you good doctrine, forsake ye, not my law.

"**The doctrine of Christ** is about righteousness, deliverances, repentance! And living abundantly in life.

Christ has taught us; the importance of the doctrine of God and how it affects our lives.

As living beings and in God's kingdom. It will be unwise for any soul or living being! That has had an encounter with Christ and his doctrine, not to abide by them or imitate him.

Abiding by the doctrine that has been laid down by Christ? Is the first principle of achieving divine destiny, purpose and living abundantly in life and living beyond the limit and limitations that may be standing between one dream and achieving in life.

In other words, there is a law that governs every event and diligence of man on earth. Nothing that came to being or be in effect in human's diligence or world that did not has a link with the law of governing.

''*Law of governing.*

Everything that is both in existence physically and spiritually? Always has a law of governing. Without a law of governing, the achievement that has been achieved in the human world? Both spiritually and physically! Would not have been achieved if the law of governing has not been properly utilized.

In other words, as the law of governing is existences in the spiritual phenomenon, also the law of governing is important in a physical phenomenon.

''*Spiritual and physical phenomenon.*

It's very important to abide by divine instructions! It's one of the elements of overcoming limits and limitations in life. For instance, not abiding by physical law! Such as, not obeying government rules or laws of a particular country or nation. Such one will be penalized and be a victim of bad law. In other words, obedience to divine law, doctrine, or instruction? Will make one a true worshipper of God and live victoriously in life.

Prayer: you will not be a victim of bad law, both! Spiritually or physically. You will live beyond the limit and limitations of life. In Jesus's name. Amen.

LIVING, BEYOND THE LIMIT! 10

"The doctrine of Christ is about righteousness, deliverance, repentance! And living abundantly in life.

(1 King 18:24). And call ye on the name of your god, and I will call on the name of the Lord, and the God that answereth by fire, let him be God. And all the people answered and said, it is well-spoken.

"**Having confidence in the resurrection power of Christ,** in all odds! Is the first sign of a true imitator of Christ and those that serve him diligently.

Maturity of the knowledge of a believer, from the word of God! And time spends in his presence is the divine grace of withstanding any form of odds and living victoriously in life.

Tremendous result or achievement of a believer in God, could not have been achieved or gained if such believers have not allowed him or themselves to be rooted or develop in the knowledge of God's word and rightly standing in faith.

God is spirit and all those that desire in living beyond the limit and limitations of life. Must serve him in spirit and in truth.

"*God is spirit! And God of righteousness.*

Prophet Elijah could not have come out boldly against the prophet of Baal if he has not first! Understand the revelation knowledge of the word and power of the most-high-God. By him be rooted in the revelation knowledge power of God, making him heavenly band! And taking authority over the prophet of Baal. He understood the authority of the God that he serves, and that gave him a divine edge in overcoming and living beyond the limit and limitations in his lifetime.

"***Revelation knowledge of the word of God.***

There is, no other way to it! Than-to-be-rooted in acquiring the revelation knowledge of God, from his word! Spending quality time in knowing him and spending time in his presences.

Heavenly band believers or imitators are those that withstand all odds and live beyond the limit and limitations of life. They are not casual believers or imitators that don't spend time in God's presence or studying his word. Heavenly band believers give all to God in knowing him.

And that gave them the divine edge in life.

Prayer: the grace to be a heavenly band believer! And taking daily authority over any odds of the enemies in Jesus's name. Amen.

LIVING, BEYOND THE LIMIT: 11

"Having confidence in the resurrection power of Christ, in all odds! Is the first sign of a true imitator of Christ, and those that serve him diligently.

(1 King 18:25). And Elijah said unto the prophets of Baal, Choose you one Bullock for yourselves, and dress it first, for ye are many and call on the name of your gods, but put no fire under.

"**Being bold in the miss of limit and limitation in life,** are the divine intervention of overcoming the operation of limit that has been hindering one success and achievement in life.

Having boldness or being bold as a believer, are a sign of the divine presence of the Holy Spirit's intervention in one life. That stood closely and guided such life, in achieving the victories over the limit and limitations that have been facing one in life.

John 16:7. Nevertheless, tell you the truth it is expedient for you that I go away, for if I go not away, the Comforter will not come unto you, but if I depart, I will send him unto you.

"*The comforter*.

The Holy Spirit is part of the Godheads that bear record in heaven! Both the father, the Son, and the Holy Spirit are one. After Jesus Christ ascended to heaven, the Godheads!

Did not leave us comfortless, he sends the Holy Spirit to teach us all things and reveal the purpose and the will of God for our lives.

Also, his! Appearances in our lives, can be related to boldness and having confidence in the revelation of the knowledge of the power of God's word.

"***His appearances, as boldness.***

No matter the operation of the limit and limitation in one life? Don't let us lose our confidence in the revelation knowledge of the power of God. Prophet Elijah understood these, and God granted him, victory in the miss of the limit and limitations that were challenging the grace of God in his lifetime.

Prayer: the comforter will guide you through your victory over

the limit and limitations in life.
In Jesus's name. Amen.

LIVING, BEYOND THE LIMIT: 12

"Being bold in the miss of limit and limitations in life, are the divine intervention of overcoming the operations of limit that has been hindering one success and achievement in life.

(1 King 18:27). And it came to pass at noon, that Elijah mocked them, and said, cry aloud for he is a god, either he is talking, or he is pursuing, or he is in a journey, or peradventure he sleepeth, and must be awaked.

"The difference between Prophet Elijah, and the prophet of Baal! Is who they lie there confident and hope with.

Achieving adequate results by Prophet Elijah at the point of limit that has been challenging his faith? Could be linked to! His confidence and hope in the living lord. Likewise, the prophet of Baal! Do depend on and have hope and confidence in their gods, but such confidence and hope they had in their gods could not enable them to live beyond the limit and limitations that surround their lives.

Meanwhile, the mystery of living beyond the limit and limitations of life, could not be adequately achieved or overcome by putting one confidence and hope in the lesser gods.

Adequate and abundant results of living beyond the limit and limitations of life all lie in putting one confidence and hope in the living Lord.

"Having confidence and hope in the living lord.

It takes daily knowing and trusting in God and living by all his instruction given from his words! That will enable anyone coming to him to live beyond the limit and limitations of life that they may be experiencing in their lifetime.

Also, having confidence and hope in God at any horrible stages of life? Is, much enough to live in total victories and live blessed in life.

"Living in total victories and living blessed.

We are all called by God to live in total victories and living in dominion in life. Any things that may want us to live below the commandments of God for our lives? These are the limit and limitations of life.

Prophet Elijah understood these! And he didn't allow such challenges to have a final say in his life he overcome them by the revelation knowledge that he has in the words of God.

Prayer: the operations of the limit and limitations of life will not have a final say in your life. You will overcome it and you will live blessed in Jesus's name. Amen.

"The difference between Prophet Elijah and the prophet of Baal! Is who they lie there confident and hope with.

(Genesis 27:3). Now therefore take. I pray thee, they bow, and go out to the filed, and take me some venison.

"**The first things first,** or the principles of living beyond the limit and limitations of life? Is, to understand the field principle and how it works! And to be a man of the field, a doer.

A doer? Can be identified as someone that does something or is occupied with things or activities that leads to substantial result or achievement. Also, a doer can be identified as someone that is involved in an activity or that renders a service to a private organization or government institution that is being rewarded for their services being rendered.

In other words, living beyond the limit and limitations of life? Involved in an understanding of a doer principle. Nothing will be achieved or obtained in life when one is not a doer! Either in services render or to seek the face of God for a particular situation in life.

"*Understanding the doer principles*.

At first, Isaac could not have beckoned on Esau for a version! If, he (Esau) was not a man of the field or someone that understood the field principles, someone that is a doer that does something.

Have an understanding of doer principles or being involved in doing something? Is the landmark of overcoming the limit and limitations of life. Also, it enables a man's destiny to move in line in every stage of life and provides victories in every endeavour of life.

"*Achieving the landmark, of! Overcoming the limit.*

We all need to be a doer! Someone that does something. Folding of arms will not enable anyone that needs victories over the limit and limitations of life. We all have to be a doer! And involved in doing something. The limit of life that anyone may be experiencing? Could be in spiritual issues or financial terms. Nothing will be achieved if one is not a doer! Either to seek the face of God with regards to the strange occurrences and issues or to do something that will lead to achieving substantial results regards to the financial issues.

Prayer: be a doer! And the substantial result will be achieved by us in Jesus's name. Amen.

"The first things first, or the principles of living beyond the limit and limitations of life? Is, to understand the field principles and how it works.

(Genesis 32:30). And Jacob called the name of the place Peniel, for I have seen God face to face, and my life is preserved.

"**To be rightly positioned, in one destiny in life** at times, having an encounter with the sources of destiny is much more important to any seeds of greatness! That need to achieve his or her purpose or destiny in life.

God! Is, the source of man's destiny and purpose in life, he endowed every seed of his with every abundant greatness in achieving in life.

Also, the limit or limitations that any seeds of God's greatness may be experienced or confronted with in life? These are all temporary not a lasting situations or challenges that may be confronting them.

In other words, at some stages of man's endeavours in life! There are always some limits or limitations that may appear visibly or confronting one purpose or challenging one ability, of achieving greatness in life.

Having the ability or acknowledging God as the source of destiny! Is the first solution to living a victorious life and overcoming the limit and limitations of life.

"*Acknowledged God as the source of destiny.*

Jacob has been experiencing the opposite direction of his destiny and purpose in his life. After what has happened between him and Esau. Due to the event that took place? He could not operate or function adequately in his destiny and purpose in life! Until a new page was open for him by God, of all sources of man's destiny in life.

"*How to function adequately in one destiny in life.*

No matter the limit and limitations any seeds of God's greatness may be experienced in life. Acknowledging God as all sources of man's destiny, is what gives way to living a victorious life and overcoming the limit and limitations of life.

Prayer: I pray in the divine encounter of God, into every area of your life! And you will achieve greatness and live beyond the limit and limitations of life. In the name of Jesus! Amen. God bless you.

LIVING, BEYOND THE LIMIT: 15

"To be rightly positioned, in one destiny in life at times? Having an encounter with the sources of destiny is much more important to any seeds of greatness.

(Genesis 33:12). And he said, let us take our journey, and let us go, and I will go before thee.

"**Progressing of men endeavour's and destiny in life**, has been designed by God to achieve the aim which it has been designed and plan from the throne of the living lord.

Every assignment of men's destiny to fulfilment can be related to the uninterrupted journey that has been seasoned with grace and favour in order to achieve its aim.

But the causes or interruption into a man's journey of fulfiling is assignment or destiny in life? Can be identified as the limit and limitations of life.

Which is capable to bring delays and hindrances into the journey of achieving one glorious destiny in life.

"Interruption towards a journey of men destiny in life.

There is always a stage or some stages of a man's journey toward fulfilling his or her utmost desired goals or success in life. But, at first! From the early stages? Everything that surrounds or involves the journey of fulfilling one utmost desire goals! May not? Be, experiencing the limit and limitations.

But at a point! The brightness of achieving or journey along with one utmost desires goal may seem to be dimming and losing the right direction of achieving.

I have a word for you! Right responses in the time of your limit and limitations are what will determine the achieving of the end result and success. But for you! You will end well and finish strong.

"Right response towards the limit and limitations of life.

It will be surprising for anyone that did not know Jacob and Esau from the time of their interruption of their destiny and diligence of their life. But knowing them when they're both on journeys towards the same direction! Will not believe the limit and limitations that they both went through in life.

Esau and Jacob utilize the right response which enables both of them to be achievers in their lifetime.

Prayer: hard work and turning to God at any stage of limit and limitations will be utilized by you. And you will achieve in life in Jesus's name. Amen.

LIVING, BEYOND THE LIMIT: 16

"Progressing of men endeavours and destiny in life, has been designed by God to achieve the aim which it has been designed and plan from the throne of the living Lord.

(Genesis 27:40). And by thy sword shalt thou live, and shalt serve thy brother, and it shall come to pass when thou shalt have the dominion, that thou shalt break his yoke off thy neck.

"**Understanding the process of** the diligence of living beyond the limit and limitations of life? Is the first principle of living blessed and living abundantly in every endeavour of life.

To understand the diligence and process of living beyond all odds? Are what enables one in turning the circumstances and challenges of limits and limitations into a stepping stone, of living victoriously and shingly beyond the limit and limitation. In other words, the first principles or first things first? Is to be diligent.

Diligences are involved in a process! And process work in hand with diligence, in achieving the end result and living abundantly.

"Diligences are involved in the process.

Every achiever of greatness or those that live abundantly in life? They have something in common! Which is that they are diligent.

Proverbs 22:29. says! Seest thou a man diligent in his business? he shall stand before kings; he shall not stand before mean men.

When one is diligent, that does not mean he or she is achieving. But the continuous diligence! Is what leads to the process of achieving and overcoming every limit and limitation of life. Esau understood! These principles and that is what make him live beyond every limit and limitation of his lifetime. He did not just be diligent in what he does, he continued with his business and that is what breaks the yoke off him.

"*Continuity in the process of diligence.*

In the record of success? Continuity is what that! Is breaking the ground of achieving. Also, continuity is the emblem of diligence and diligence involved in the process.

Every candidate of success or those that wish to live beyond every limit and limitation of life? Should be diligent and understand the process of continuity in diligence.

Prayer: by understanding all these principles? You will live strong and you will overcome every limit and limitation of life in Jesus's name. Amen.

LIVING, BEYOND THE LIMIT: 17

"Understanding the process, the diligence of living beyond the limit and limitations of life? Is the first principle of living blessed and living abundantly in every endeavour of life.

(Genesis 1:26). And God said, let us make man in our image, after our likeness, and let them have dominion over every creeping thing that creepeth upon the earth.

"**The mandate of God to every man living under the surface of the heavens?** Is to have dominion and to live beyond every limit and limitation of life.

Our dominion has been put in place and ordained by God before any man was giving birth to-in-life. Also, the dominion that has been ordained by God? Has been included in our purpose package before gaining our consciousness as a being or arriving on the surface of the earth.

In other words, we have been mandated by God to live in dominion and living beyond every limit and limitation that may be standing between us and our purpose fulfilment.

"***Mandated to live in dominion.***

The current or present challenges of our lives? Does not determine our God-giving destiny or purpose in life.

Whatever circumstances or challenges that we may be facing with? Are just interruptions to our God-giving ordained purpose and destiny in life! Such, don't have the capacity or authority to determine our purpose or destiny.

In other words, at any space or time in our lives? That may seem worrisome or challenging! Let us remember that we have been mandated by God to live in dominion and to live beyond every limit and limitation of life.

By we have the awareness? We will be able to connect to God's divine victory plan for our lives, and tell the limit and limitations standing between us and our diligence in life! Where they belong.

"*Awareness, the key to! Total victory.*

Being aware, or acknowledging the mandate and promises of God, from his word for our lives? Is the first priority of achieving divine purpose and standing strong in the miss of the limit. Also, awareness is the key to success and achievement in life. In other words, being aware or able to be aware of the promises and who we are in God? Is, the first stage of moving close to our destiny and purpose achieving.

Prayer: the grace to be aware of the promises and the greatness of God into your life today and beyond in Jesus's name. Amen.

LIVING, BEYOND THE LIMIT! 18

"The mandate of God to every man living under the surface of heaven? Is to have dominion and to live beyond every limit and limitation of life.

(Genesis 17:4). As for me, behold, my covenant is with thee, and thou shalt be a father of many nations.

"**The essential platform of launching out a man's destiny in life? Is** to be recognized in the divine purpose plan of God.

The divine purpose plan of God? Is the divine platform that has been designed by

God! To launch out every child of destiny in life, to their divine purpose and destiny. Also, the divine purpose plan of God? Can also be referred as to God's covenant between God and every carrier of destiny.

Destiny? Is, more than! The reasons and purpose of men-existences but destiny is the total package of every being living on the surface of heaven. In other words, living beyond the limit and limitations of one destiny in life? Is to be recognized in the divine platform purpose plan of God.

"Divine platform purpose plan.

God is the God of knowledge, abundant and the only reliable source to every achievement of destiny and purpose. Also, he knows! He has the secret and solution of every carrier of destiny and their purpose in life.

It will be unwise for anyone that thought the achievements and secrets to their purpose driving goals and destiny lie with what they have known and with the knowledge they have! But, every solution and secret to one destiny and purpose in life lies with God.

"*Acknowledged God.*

Abram was a skilful hunter that was highly dedicated to his hunter business and diligent in what he loved to do best. To him and everyone that surrounds him? May have concluded that! That is what he was born for and that is his destiny and purpose in life.

Until God of destiny and purpose reviews his destiny and purpose to him.

Prayer: may you be continuously remembered in

the divine purpose plan of God for your life in Jesus's name. Amen.

LIVING, BEYOND THE LIMIT: 19

"The essential platform of launching out a man's destiny in life? Is to be recognized in the divine purpose plan of God.

(Genesis 18:1). And the Lord appeared unto him in the plains of Mamre and he sat in the tent door in the heat of the day.

"**At times,** figuring out of some strange mysteries and all strange circumstances that surround it! Maybe a fathom of wonder and understanding of beliefs its existence.

But to the little of our understanding in solving and approaching the elements of the solution, regard to the strange happening or mysteries, will always leave us with effortless achievements and little time in approaching important goals and visions for our lives.

No matter, how equipped we are in information and well established in solving a situation? If the strange mystery is beyond our ability to solve, it can never be solved by us, no matter how established we are in the information and solving plan.

In other words, living beyond the limit and limitations of life? Are the divine approaches from the throne of God, which is divine! To the natural existence of men living on the surface of the earth, for supernatural intervention of overcoming strange mysteries, and living beyond every limit and limitation of life.

"*Supernatural intervention*.

Whatever that is beyond the natural? Can only be approached or solved by supernatural intervention! Where God inhabits the praise of his people and divinely intervenes in their unsolvable circumstances or challenges that may be questioning their faith and stand in the living God that they serve.

Also, in times of strange mysteries or challenges? Where one seeks solutions matters a lot. Solution seeking outside the presence of God will! But, only add more strange manifestations and prolong one divine intervention of God for a lasting and healthy solution.

"*Where seating in terms of strange mysteries*.

In times of Abram's strange mysteries? The Bible identified or informed us that he sat on the tent door, despite how intense the weather was. He didn't allow himself to be found or join some strange company or seek help outside the plan and purpose of God for his life. The solution or solving plan to the strange mysteries of his life met him, where he was seating. The place of our seating is much more important in the time of strange circumstances and mysteries of a fathom of our understanding.

Prayer: you will be rightly positioned in the time of your strange circumstances and mysteries of your life! In the name of Jesus. Amen.

LIVING, BEYOND THE LIMIT: 20

"At times, figuring out of some strange mysteries, and all strange circumstances that surround it! Maybe a fathom of wonder and understanding of beliefs its existence.

(Psalm 27:1). The Lord is my light and my salvation; whom shall I fear? The Lord is the strength of my life, of whom shall I be afraid.

"**Acknowledging who God is** to us! And with the strength of his might, the Majesty of his glory gives us all reasons of giving him all honour and glory every day of our lives.

The living Lord is the light of our salvation and the one that is saving us from all odds and mysteries that are beyond the fathom of our understanding and enabling us in achieving lasting victory at every horrible event that may be questioning our beliefs and faith in the strength of his might.

No matter, how strange or circumstances the mysteries of the limit to your success and progress in life may seem! The Lord is your salvation and is capable enough of helping you, living beyond the limit and limitations of your life.

"The Lord is my light and my salvation.

There are no other victories that you may desire to achieve or salvation that may be much more needed to you than the one that you have obtained in Christ Jesus. He is your light and the salvation of your souls! The strength of your life.

In other words, having this knowledge of who God is to you? You should any longer be a victim or servant to fear or the operation of the limit and limitations that may be standing between you and your achievements, progress, and success in life.

"I acknowledge you Lord you are the strength of my life.

The battle is of the Lord, anyone that thought! The battle of living beyond the limit and limitations of life? Can be won or defeated by one strength! Such one is just planning to lose the battle even before launching out His weaponry arsenal.

The battle is of the lord he is the one that will fight your battle, and he his, the strength of your life. Yahweh – Nissi.

Prayer: victories over every battle your life, maybe experiencing at this moment and I pray! The hand of Yahweh - Nissi upon you in Jesus's name. Amen.

LIVING, BEYOND THE LIMIT! 21

"Acknowledging who God is, to us! And with the strength of his might, the majesty of his glory! Gives us, all reasons for giving him all honours and glory in every day of our lives.

(Ecclesiastes 9:11). I returned and saw under the sun, that the race is not to the swift, nor the battle to the strong, neither yet bread to the wise, nor yet riches to men of understanding, nor yet favour to men of skill, but time and chance happeneth to them all.

"**Time is highly important** and is one of the essential attributes of overcoming any form of odds and living beyond the limit and limitations of life.

The way we utilize our time and what we invest our time into is also much more important to anyone that desires of becoming an overcomer and living in success, achieving one vision and goals in life. Not properly, making use of one time? Either to involve oneself in reading, listing to some faith teaching, seeking God's face in prayers and joining other faith-minded believers in some Christian activities on social media, social gathering, winning souls for Christ or even learning some skills and having some knowledge in where one has been experiencing the limit, be an overcomer or living beyond the limit? Will always be mountainous challenges to anyone that refuses to make proper use of his or her time.

''Understanding the timing.

We all need time, the horrible circumstances or the challenges to our achievements, some of it! Maybe a foundational which the onset of it, was not known to you or the mysteries may be, without your consent or it occurred at a particular time.

Did you know? All the strange mysteries of your life might have occurred at a particular timing or a foundational challenge. The solution of it will eventually take place or occurred at a set time or divine timing.

''The set time and divine timing.

The timing of God is either set or divine! Are all working alongside in liberating us from all that has been holding our destiny down or causing us to be living at the limit of life?

Also, when the set and the divine of the timing of God! Take charge of a particular situation or a mountainous circumstance, nothing can have held back the hand of God for a lasting solution.

Prayer: your set and divine timing of liberation of living beyond all limits and limitations of life! Is, here in the name of Jesus. And you will live abundantly in the name of Jesus. Amen.

LIVING, BEYOND THE LIMIT! 22

"Time is highly important! And is one of the essential attributes of overcoming any form of odds and living beyond the limit and limitations of Life.

(Ecclesiastes 12:13). Let us hear the conclusion of the whole matter; fear God, and keep his commandments, for this is the whole duty of man.

"**There is no other way**, that can substitute or neglect the standard way of healthy living in God and in one life! Than-the-one that has been laid and established in the word of God.

The fear of the Lord is the beginning of wisdom. Not that those that choose the Godly way of life and living by Godly instructions are those without knowledge, or know what to do at times?

Every obedience to the Godly way of life or living is what can be regarded as wisdom and the whole duty of man. Is, the duty of every soul living under the surface of life! To obey the commandments of their creators, the living Lord, the creators of heaven and earth, and the maker of men.

In other words, achieving the success of living beyond the limit, can also be obtained! When one is living in the obedience of God and having the fear of God in one Life.

"The fear of the Lord, is the beginning of wisdom.

Every habitat living under the surface of Life needs to fear God. Also, the fear of God is the beginning of wisdom, and it can be regarded as one of the attributes of living success in Life.

Living in the success or being an achiever some time, did not relate or related to what we have acquired in terms of skills or knowledge gained.

But the secret to success at times lies with how instructed we are in God and how we allow the fear of God to have its way and dominated our being.

''The fear of the Lord, path the way for successful living.

Have you been dominated by your worries and the reasons why some things are not working the way you desired or plan them to be? Let's do some examinations now! How instructed are we in Godly instructions? If our finding indicates or reviews that we are not living in a Godly way of life or the fear of God cannot be discovered in our lives is a sign of the reasons for our worries and how some things in our lives are not working the way we have always been, desire and wanted it to be achieved. Also, it can be the reason for our limits in Life.

Prayer: the grace to abide and live Godly in Life and the grace to be dominated by the fear of

God into your life in Jesus's name. Amen.

LIVING, BEYOND THE LIMIT! 23

"There is no other way, that can substitute or neglect the standard way of healthy living in God and in one Life. Than-the-one that has been said and established in the word of God.

(Ecclesiastes 12:14). For God will bring every deed into judgment, including every hidden thing, whether it is good or evil.

"**What we profess to be,** and our standard of living in God's word in articulated our victories in living beyond the limit of Life is, essentially important in giving us lasting victories beyond every odd and limit of Life.

The word of God is the standard and measures that instructed every true believer that daily seeks him in knowing his mind and with the application of overcoming mysteries and the standard of living.

We need the word of God in our daily lives, giving our time to know more of his word? Is, the start of gaining access to his presence and having the divine edge over whatever that may seem unsolvable and unachievable to us in the time of our difficulties.

Also, praise stands as weaponry of liberation on the spiritual battlefield! Likewise, our deep knowledge and more intake of God's word in our lives, Give us access to victories and liberation in the time of our spiritual battlefield.

''The measures of standard living in God's word.

Abiding by divine instruction and living rightly is also much more important in living victoriously in Life and enjoying every benefit in God's kingdom. At times, our obedience and how instructed we are? These are what gave us the divine step of overcoming and living beyond every limit and limitation of Life.

''Divine step of overcoming every limit and limitations of Life.

Truly God will judge every hidden thing, whether good or evil. In other words, every work of men! Will be judged by God.

It's not the mind of God for the strange mysteries of limits and limitations that any one of his maybe experience in Life or at present. But our duties as true believers of God that imitate him and seek him daily in our lives, is to abide by his Godly way of living and yield to every instruction given from his word.

By us yielding to all his way, every strange mystery, limit and limitation of Life will be a forgotten battle and we will live victoriously at all times.

Prayer: the divine grace from the throne of God for Godly living into your life! And the divine grace for successful achievement in every area of your life. In Jesus's name. Amen.

LIVING, BEYOND THE LIMIT! 24

"What we profess to be, and our standard of living in God's word in articulated our victories in living beyond the limit of Life? Is, essentially important, in giving us lasting victories beyond every odd and limit of Life.

(Song of Solomon 2:1). I am the rose of Sharon and the lily of the valley.

"**Songs are the melody that sweetest deep into the souls,** and each of every song that human listing to or that cross into the hearing of men are a very powerful instrument that heals the souls of men and makes human hearts to be merry.

Songs have meaning! At times, some songs cross the hearing of men. Some may not be well understood, but the tone and sound of it! Makes the heart and souls of men to be merry, even though it does not have wording meaning, due to the languages being used to compose the song.

Also, as songs used in human's social endeavours! Likewise, songs are also being used in praising God and thanking him for his wondrous act and his blessings in human lives.

Overcoming every limit and limitation of life can also be attributed to using praises songs, to worship God, when the limit and limitations of Life are pointing battle of challenges and difficulties in one way and Life.

''Using's praises songs, to God in time of the limit.

The mysteries of songs are beyond human's methodology of reasons. Songs have been highly active before the time of creation! Songs are heavenly activities in giving praises and adoration to the most-high God.

In other words, songs has been used in human social endeavours and giving praises to God who is worthy of our praises. Also, songs of praise are spiritual weaponry of liberation on the time of spiritual battlefield.

''The mysteries of songs, it's beyond human's methodology.

Songs gave a meaningful meaning to the human's social gathering and gave praises to God in his presence. Without songs in human social activities or in God's presence? Tremendous progress and achievements in human lives would not have been achieved! If songs are missing in human endeavours.

Meanwhile, King Solomon can be related as one that lives beyond his limit and limitations in his Lifetime and used songs as an instrument of victory.

Prayer: song of victories will be used by you in your time of limit and limitations of your life in Jesus'S name. Amen.

LIVING, BEYOND THE LIMIT! 25

"Songs are the melody that sweetest deep into the souls, and each of every song that human listing to or that cross into the hearing of men? Are very powerful instruments.

(Songs of Solomon 2:11). For, lo the winter is past, the rain is over and gone.

"**In the previous series 16!** When I was discussing the limit and limitations that Esau went through in his lifetime? In Genesis 27:40.

From that vantage point, he came to terms with the unimaginable fathom of reasons!

And with the unimaginable of his understanding? To figure out his unawareness of all the circumstances that were before him in his father's presence.

Did we know? During his process of having or achieving dominion in his unaware circumstances? Did he encounter (He encountered) the seasons of winter, summer, springs, and lots of rainfall? But the word of his father "Isaac" came to be fulfilled in his Life and he live beyond his limit and limitation.

I don't know the seasons you have encountered in the process of overcoming the limit and limitations of your Life! I have a word for you today! In the season, either winter, summer, spring, or the seasons of rainfall. You will live beyond the limit and limitations of your life.

''*Living beyond your limit.*

There is one thing that is so important in any process! Either in overcoming, achieving and living in victories or acquiring important knowledge? Diligences and readiness of achieving are some of the processes that earnest the victory path to everyone that is in a process of achieving greatness and abundant result.

All these were understood by Esau! And he utilizes the process that was available to him in the time of his difficulties, and he has a blissful ending.

"*Utilizing available process in the time of your limit and limitation.*

As Esau utilize the available process that was available to him? Which makes him-have-a blissful ending. Also, there is always an available process in any of the limits and limitations that you may be encountering in life.

In the next series! More light will be shared on the more important process that will make you live beyond your limit and limitations of Life.

Prayer: I pray in! Great success and achievements in every area of your life in Jesus's name. Amen.

LIVING, BEYOND THE LIMIT! 26

"During the limit and limitations that Esau went through, he encounters the seasons of winter, summer, springs, and a lot of rainfall. But the word of his father "Isaac" came to be fulfilled in his life.

"**Achievement is one of great voluminous in the millennium century,** and it has been a great measure that defined great achiever's in our present world. Has anyone, ever think or thought? How important is it to be a great achiever in this present day and to be an influential personality in the atmosphere of great achievers?

"**All this information** was discovered by Esau, and he was well informed about the entire important tool that needed to be an achievement. Not that he was well educated or either was he well learned, but there is something in him that is so unique, that is beyond human knowledge and wisdom, which cannot be on the same equal with human ability. Which, is known as the "Spirit of dominion.

In Job 32:8-9. But there is a spirit in man and the inspiration of the Almighty giveth them understanding, vs9. Great men are not always wise neither do the aged understand judgment.

''*As a hunter.*

Only little does he know! Not to be available in the area of his speciality, because, he has spent his whole life learning a particular skill, which is a hunter! And he was good at what he has acquired.

Am speaking to you today! Your enemies might have stolen your belonging and valuable things, but they cannot steal your dream.

Prayer: I prophesied by the spirit of dominion, whatever you might have lost, you will recover all and overtake in the name of Jesus. Amen.

LIVING, BEYOND THE LIMIT! 27

"Achievement is one of great voluminous in the millennium century, and it has been a great measure that defined great achiever's in our present world.

(Exodus 31:2-3). See I have called by name Bezaleel the son of Uri, the son Hur, of the tribe of Judah vs3. And I have filled him with the spirit of God, in wisdom, and in understanding, and in knowledge, and in all manner of workmanship.

"**There is always** some blissful uniqueness that is beyond all human's imagination! That has been divinely gifted by God to all human beings that ever live on this surface of the earth.

This blissful uniqueness or gifted endowment from the creators of heaven and earth can be related to skills and divine abilities.

Likewise, as, some skills! Are divinely gifted by God, also! Some skills can be acquired or learned from various academic institutions. There is, also! Some skills, that one can always have access to, in order to live beyond some form of limit and limitations that may be standing, in one way of successful living on earth.

Meanwhile, without the consent or the space of skills availability in humans lives? Surrounding in all humans environment would not have beautifully access and live in.

''*Beautifully access and live in.*

The importance of skills is like a boxer in a boxing ring that fights his or her opponent! In a boxing challenge, that's defeated his opponent in a boxing competition. The opponent that was been defeated? Could be, related to! As circumstances, limits, and challenges that stood strongly against every availability of achieving and successful living in Life.

In other words, the boxers can be related to you! Or anyone that desires to live beyond every limit and limitation of life that defeated his or her opponent.

''*Defeating your opponent.*

Esau defeated his limit and limitations by his skills and by understanding the revelation knowledge showcased to him by his father

"Isaac" That when thou shall have the dominion that this YOKE will be broken off you.

And by the combination of his skills, with the revelations knowledge of living beyond the limit and limitations? He achieved success.

As the skills acquired by you may not be enough? But with the combinations of the revelations knowledge that has been impacted to you! In this series. You will live beyond the limit and limitations of your life.

Prayer: in your process of achieving in the miss of your limit and limitations of Life! Outstanding testimony will be achieved by you. In Jesus's name. Amen.

LIVING, BEYOND THE LIMIT! 28

"There is always some blissful uniqueness that beyond all humans' imaginations, that has been divinely gifted by God.

(Exodus 31:6). *Moreover, I have appointed Oholiab son of Ahisamak, of the tribe of Dan, to help him. Also, I have given the ability to all the skilled workers to make everything I have commanded you.*

"**The importance of skills is much important that determines between the process of every human's abilities to live beyond any elements that may surround or involved any limit or limitations,** that may be standing between achieving and not being able to achieve.

At times, the edge of victories or liberation! That most humans, maybe longing to acquired or obtained in any situation? Does not involved or surrounded in some mechanism but is involved in the mechanism of having a skill.

Have skills or acquire some skills? Are the rightful tools of the mechanism of achieving lasting and suitable victories over every limit and limitation that may seem like an unachievable phenomenon in life?

''*Unachievable phenomenon of life*.

Without skill or not been in the process of acquiring one? Life will always be an unachievable phenomenon at any stage of life.

The importance of skills is so highly important that God endowed Bezaleel, the son of Uri, and Oholiab son of Ahisamak not for self-benefit but for the use of humanity and to give a rightful meaningful meaning to every human's world and its surrounding.

"Humans world and its surrounding.

Those that know, the importance of skills or that use skills in a time of horrible challenges or circumstances? Was Esau! That embraced his hunter skills and gave him liberations in the miss of all odds and difficulties of his life. How could the journey of overcoming the limit and limitations of "He" Esau! Be, if he didn't have hunter skills in the first place.

The process of his liberations could be a mirage and nothing could have supported the grace of his father upon him if he didn't have hunter as a skill.

Prayer: I pray in the grace to be fruitful in skills acquired by you. In the name of Jesus. Amen.

LIVING, BEYOND THE LIMIT! 29

"The importance of skills is much important that determine between the process of every human's abilities to live beyond any element.

(Proverbs 8:8). Doth not wisdom cry? and understanding put forth her voice?

"**Wisdom will ever be! The cutting edge to live in victories in life**, and the great element that links to every intellectual ability of men.

Wisdom is that application of knowledge that is involved in the understanding of things! How it forms and is made. Everything that is well visible or occurred in the human world? Has is form and how they are being made.

Meanwhile, without? Not typing or giving space to the splendours element that is linked to human's intellectual abilities, which is known! As wisdom, the application of knowledge that carried understanding in the area of discovering, and with the ability to disband every limit and limitation of life! Will only left one, longing for a solution at every endeavour of humans inabilities of discovering a lasting solution.

''*Inabilities of discovering*.

Nothing will be! In one time or season of the limit and limitations of life, when one is not typing or giving space to the splendours of recipes that are involved in humans intellectuals' abilities to discover in the time of one limit and limitations! Which is known?

As wisdom, knowledge, and understanding. But there is! Inbuilt of human's abilities to discover, which is built in humans intellectual abilities, which is known as? Instinct.

Instincts are not acquired or learned in any institutions! But are divine abilities that God gave humans a cutting edge in terms of horrible occurrences.

''*Your instinct*.

Your instinct? Is, also! One of the splendours elements of winning over your limit and inabilities of achieving your desired success and goals that you may have set or longing to achieve in life.

No matter? How strategic the operations of your limit in life may seem? Having this entire splendours element! Will always tell your limit and limitations to back off! From you.

Prayer: every limit and limitation of your life! Will give way, and success, unachievable goals will be achieved by you. In Jesus's name. Amen.

LIVING, BEYOND THE LIMIT! 30

"Wisdom, will ever be! The cutting edge to live in victories in life, and the great element that links to every intellectual ability of men.

(Proverbs 2:3). Yea, if thou criest after knowledge, and liftest up thy voice for understanding.

"**Humans will ever belonging for their space of inabilities of gaining access to their utter must dream** and with the reasons of not acquiring the most success between the immediate materialization of their target vision and why much limit and limitations still hovering over their imagination of fathoming adequately solution of the reasons of visible mystery occurrence's.

As a knowledge, has been known as a fact! That nothing in the human world can distinguish this eloquent accessibility of winning over any limit that may be visible in humans lives. Likewise, knowledge paths the way from searching to discovering, and from discovering to achieving the result of living over the limit and limitations of life.

''*Knowledge paths the way! From searching to discovering.*

What is the real meaning of knowledge? From the dictionary point of view! Knowledge is a fact. Information and skills acquired through experience or education, the theoretical or practical understanding of a subject. Meanwhile, knowledge built the human world and adequately gives tremendous meaning to humans societies, and their environments.

Also, without acquiring knowledge, either to be skilled! In terms of human challenges, that may be experiencing the responsibilities of any human being living on the surface of the earth, or acquiring knowledge in God's word! With regard to being close to God or what his words are saying to all unimaginable limits and strange occurrences that one may be experiencing within life! Limits will only give way when one has been well informed in skills.

''*Knowledge needs to be acquired.*

Knowledge is different from Instinct! Instinct is a heavenly endowment built into every human being that is living on the surface of the earth, is not learned, like knowledge! But is built by God in humans for having a cutting edge in time of the limit and limitations of life.

Also, Instinct! Due to its cutting edge? It also helps when one is in need of knowledge in terms of making choices, either in the area of academics or what to engage in life. As wisdom, Instinct is cutting edge over every strange occurrence! Likewise, knowledge is also a cutting edge in living a blessed life.

Prayer: wisdom, Instinct, and knowledge will path the way to your success living in life. In Jesus's name. Amen.

LIVING, BEYOND THE LIMIT! 31

"Humans will ever be! Longing for their space of inabilities of gaining access to their uttermost dreams and with the reasons of not acquiring the most success between their immediate materialization.

(Proverbs 4:4). For I give you good doctrine, forsake ye, not my law.

There are principles that are involved in living beyond the limit and limitations that any living being, may want to achieve at any space of time. As having-a-skill with some recipes that I have mentioned in the previous pages? Also, be obedient to the mandate that has been laid down by our Lord Jesus Christ! Before ascending to heaven, is also most important to everyone who has been longing and wanted to live beyond every limit and limitation of life.

The doctrine that has been laid down by our Lord Jesus Christ? Is about righteousness, repentance, and seeking God's kingdom.

Matthew 6:33. says! Seek ye first the kingdom of heaven and his righteousness, and all these things shall be added unto thee.

"*Seek ye first, the kingdom of heaven.*

To seek ye! Is about obedience to the heavenly doctrine mandate that has been divinely given in order for every follower of

Christ to live beyond their limit in their various lives.

Also, obedient can also be grouped or attributed as one of the instruments to use, over every limitation and limit that one may be challenged with.

In other words, **ALL THESE THINGS!** Can be referred to, as those things, we are managing or failing to overcome or achieved. Such as? Some recurrence, issues or projects that, that-may-seem unachievable and impossible for materialization.

Also, **ALL THESE THINGS!** Can be some health issues or challenges that have been demanding lots of our earnings and income. I have a word for you today! By you living to divine doctrine and mandate that has been divinely laid down by Christ Jesus? I see you living beyond all your limit and limitations of your life in Jesus's name.

''*Living beyond your limit.*

Living, beyond your limit! Is possible to achieve if one allows his or herself to follow the recipes that have been given and adequately be a doer of it. Whatever cannot be solved or achieved! In terms of living beyond one limit? Such does not exist! On this planet that was formed and created by God.

If I and you, truly believe that this earth? Is laid, formed, and created by God! Let's be assured and confident that? No matter how highly or lowly the limit and limitation maybe? It can be solved by God and achieved when we live to the recipes of materialization.

Prayer: In this season! Great things will be done and achieved by you in Jesus's name. Amen.

LIVING, BEYOND THE LIMIT! 32

"There are principles that are involved in living beyond the limit and limitation that any living being, may want to achieve at any space of time.

(Matthew 6:33). Seek ye first the kingdom of heaven and his righteousness, and all these things shall be added unto thee.

"**Having mentioned skills,** wisdom, Instinct, knowledge, and obedience to divine mandate in the previous series? There is a need to talk about the divine mandate that will enable any individual or collectives that are in need of living beyond every limit and limitation that they may be experiencing at any stage of life.

Seeking the kingdom of God, or to seek God's kingdom? Is continuous obedience for every soul in Christ, not when wish or want to obey the heavenly divine instruction given to every living soul that in Christ.

Also, living to the commandments! In seeking a heavenly kingdom? There is an important aspect that is involved in kingdom seeking, which is righteousness! One may be obedient to the heavenly mandate which is to seek the kingdom and not be obedient to the other aspect which is righteousness.

Meanwhile, one may be obedient to righteousness that is involved in seeking the heavenly kingdom and not obedient to the other aspect which is the kingdom.

''*The kingdom and righteousness.*

These two divine mechanisms are the heavenly requirement in achieving our desired vision and goals for living beyond the limit and limitations and achieving our desired dreams that we might have not been able to set before the beginning of the year.

Is graciously important for any individual or collective in living beyond the limit of life. As have said that **ALL THESE THINGS!** Can be referred to as those things that we are managing or failing to overcome or achieved! Such as some re-occurrences, issues, or projects that may seem unachievable and impossible for materialization.

''*Shall be added unto thee.*

When we have well able to understand the two mechanisms that are involved in the kingdom seeking and adequately carrying it out in our daily lives? Then **ALL THESE THINGS!** Shall be added unto us.

In other words, when we are being obedient to the two important keys? Of receiving our blessings from the throne of God! The limit and limitations of life will be a forgotten story.

Prayer: I pray in the grace to live in obedience at every stage and endeavour of your life in Jesus's name. Amen.

LIVING, BEYOND THE LIMIT! 33

"Seeking the kingdom of God, or to seek God's kingdom? Is a continuous obedient for every soul in Christ.

(John 3:16). For God so loved the world, that he gave his only begotten son, that whosoever believeth in him should not perish, but have everlasting life.

"**Is the divine will of God,** for every diligent in righteousness and obedient to the heavenly kingdom! That? They live beyond every limit and limitation of life.

This enables God to come to the world in form of man! Not to rule in the human world or to serve him? He came that everyone in God is divinely placed and endowed in the area of achieving their assignment on earth and bringing every soul back to God. Christ has paid the price between utilizing one purpose and not being able to utilize one purpose in life.

Achieving this great success of living beyond one limit? Lies in having Christ as one source and living to all his commandments in his word.

''Living to all his commandments.

Every believer in Christ needs to live to all instructions given in the word of God! No matter how one is diligent in prayers? If one is not obedient to instruction or divine mandate? It will be difficult for one to achieve the success of living beyond one limitation in life.

In other words, let us be diligent in our prayers and live all obedience giving in the word of God.

''*Living in obedience to God's word.*

There is no other way to do it! Than-to-live in obedience to God's word. At times, due to one rightly position in obedience and righteousness? Some strange mystery that we see as challenging will be defeated! Due to one rightly position in righteousness and obedience.

Also, righteousness and obedience strengthen the relationship between God and men and help them to know the mind of God to some strange mysteries that they may be experiencing in life.

Prayer: the grace to be in obedience and to live in righteousness in Jesus's name. Amen.

LIVING, BEYOND THE LIMIT! 34

"Is the divine will of God, for every diligent in righteousness and obedient to the heavenly kingdom! That? They live beyond every limit and limitation of life.

(Proverbs 8:17). I love those who love me, and those who seek me diligently will find me.

"**At any stage or time in life?** Whether at any season of the year; winter, spring, or summer or when things are good or opposite? Finding and seeking after the living lord! Should be our main priority.

Not what we see as easily to clave to or what people around us are doing. That which some have been yielding to tremendous results and success! Which is not the mind of God for us to seek after.

Seeking after God or finding him? Are divine treasure, which enables every diligently to the divine obedient, that connects one with heavenly resources that are stored in the divine treasures to those that find and seek after God.

Also, every obedient to the divine instruction? Always carry the grace of God to those that yield to the divine instruction and guide them to acquired solutions in the time of every limit and limitations of life that may come across their way or path in life.

''*Your path has been guided by God.*

There is no quality of time that has been spent in finding or seeking after God! That is of waste of time. Every of our diligence in the kingdom of God! Are divine mechanism or divine grace that has been divinely placed during our time of seeking and finding God? That helps us in the time that we thought some strange limit or limitations that we encounter would have swallowed up one at a glance.

But glory be to God! For our obedience and victories.

''*Your obedient and victories.*

Obedient is one of the great mechanisms of the solution to the strange mysteries that we may ever experience or encounter in life.

Some limits that we may think of as mountainous and time-consuming? Yielding to obedient and following all divine instructions given in the scripture are healthy in having a lastly victories and defeating all the lies of the enemies.

Prayer: I pray in the grace to seek after God in all times of your life in the name of Jesus. Amen.

LIVING, BEYOND THE LIMIT! 35

"At any stage or time in life? Whether at any season! Of the year: winter, spring, or summer or when things are good or opposite? Finding and seeking after the living lord! Should be our main priority.

(1 Chronicle 12:32). Of the son of Issachar who had understanding of the times, to know what Israel ought to do, their chiefs were two hundred, and all their brethren at their command.

"**In living beyond every limit and limitations of life,** there are always some elements which can be simply referred to as mechanisms that will enable or give one advantage when the limit of life is pointing to a challenging battle in one way or life.

Time is also one of the greatest elements or mechanisms that can easily enable one to have a victory edge for overcoming every limit and limitation of life. With proper use of one time, either in finding God or being trained where one has been experiencing the limit of life? Limits and limitations of life will always be a cloud of dust to be cleaned from one way and path of achieving success in one life.

''*Limit and limitations, as a cloud of dust.*

Any things that may be standing between you and your progress in life, or limit and limitations that may seem like mysteries of fathoming solutions! And such is beyond one capable of achieving, can all be referred to as a cloud of **dust** that needs to be cleaned from one path and ways in life.

As we all have known! A dusty road is not a healthy place to be or be around! Reasons, been to the effect that it can cause one health and damaging one cloth.

We need to do away with any dusty elements and cleanse ourselves from any dust that can put our lives at the limit of life.

"*Cleaning the dust*.

After understanding the previous elements or mechanisms that have been mentioned in the previous series? Understanding one time and how to utilize it! In order for achieving a lasting victory over the limit and limitations of life is encouraging important to everyone that desires to live beyond every limit of life.

Prayer: the proper understanding of time and utilizing it, in time of any limit and limitations! That may come across your path in life in Jesus's name. Amen.

LIVING, BEYOND THE LIMIT! 36

"In living beyond every limit and limitations of life, there are always some elements which can be simply referred to as mechanisms.

(Isaiah 1:19). If you are willing and obedient, you will eat the good things of the land.

"**Willingness and obedience** are also one of the mechanisms of achieving the result of living beyond every limit and limitation of life.

Without not having an act of courage or zeal in any things in life? Achieving or solving the situation or circumstances will always be mysteries in one unimaginable of solving.

We all need these great instruments of achieving the result over every limit of life which is been known as willingness and obedience.

Also, to be willing and obedient? Are one of the signs of a true imitator of Christ that diligently obey the commandments of Christ and lives to all his instructions.

Without not allowing oneself into this great solution plan? One will always wonder fathoming how to live beyond every circumstance that life maybe throws at one.

''To be willing and obedient are one of the signs of true imitators of Christ.

No matter how the challenges, the limit and limitations of life may be! Being an imitator of Christ? Distinguished between those that imitate Christ and those that serve him not.

In other words, imitators of Christ have already been given the cutting edge in terms of their willingness and obedience in the instructed obedience that has been instructed by Christ for every follower of him. And those that imitate or follow Christ? Has been giving the grace, power, anointing, and favour to overcome the limit of life.

''*Overcoming your limit.*

No one can wage the war of overcoming the battles of the limit and limitations of life for us. Everyone has been giving grace on every journey of life in making proper utilizing and living blessed in life.

But, what makes the difference between those that achieved the result and those that achieved it not? Is the ability of been willing and obedient. We all need these two mechanisms if we really want to live beyond every limit and limitation of life.

Prayer: the grace to be willing and obedient in your life in the name of Jesus. Amen.

LIVING, BEYOND THE LIMIT! 37

"Willingness and obedience, are also one of the mechanisms of achieving the result of living beyond every limit and limitationsof life.

(Matthew 6:7). And when you pray, do not use vain repetitions as the heathen do. For they think that they will be heard for their many words.

"Prayer is also one of the elements or mechanisms that can enable or help us in living beyond every limit and limitations of life.

The importance of prayers, in the lives of every believer in Christ, enables or helps us to achieve destiny's purpose, and win every battle that we may confront in life.

Looking at it! Before the dispensations of the Holy Spirit? The prophet of old and those that serve God in spirit and obedient! Understood the wonderful importance of prayers and how it gives their lives a meaningful meaning. Without prayers or the use of prayers? Great accomplishments and success that have been recorded by the prophet of old and in the dispensations of the Holy Spirit would not have been recorded! If prayers have not been in place.

"*What is the real meaning of prayers?*

As every meaningful substance that we may ever experience or have in contact within our environments or that we used. As a meaning! Likewise, prayers signified the true imitators of Christ.

Let's look at it! Few meanings of prayers.

- Prayer is a miss of communication between God and men.
- Prayer is a miss of receiving from God.
- Prayer is a miss of talking to God.

"*The requirements for prayers*.

As the word prayers is a great tool in the lives of every believer in Christ! Which serves him diligently and obeys his instructions and commandments? The first principle to being a praying believer is? By accepting Lord Jesus Christ as Lord and saviour.

As is always known that a prayer-less believer is a powerless believer. Prayers enable purpose fulfilment and destiny achievement.

Limits and limitations of life will not give way to one life! If one is not a praying believer and has a unique understanding of the importance of prayers.

Prayer. I pray in the oil and grace of prayers into your life in these seasons and beyond in Jesus's name. Amen.

LIVING, BEYOND THE LIMIT! 38

"Prayers are also one of the elements or mechanisms that can enable or help us in living beyond every limit and limitations of life.

(Psalm 20:7). Some trust in chariots, and some in horses.

"**After understanding all the elements that can make us achieve our uttermost victory over the limit and limitations of our lives?** Having a proper understanding of who we lie our trust and hope with within any time of odds and strange circumstances that may be falling our lives? Is also one of the mechanisms of living beyond the limit and limitations of our lives.

In the previous series! I do mention prayers as one of the elements or mechanisms that can enable us to have success in the miss of any hindrances or horrible challenges.

And I gave some important meaning of prayer! Prayers are always divine tools for every believer in Christ. It does not matter when we came to Christianity or gave our lives to Christ. The moment we accept Lord Jesus Christ! As our Lord and personal saviour? The power and grace to command and communicate to God have already been activated in our Christianity journey.

Also, I will give other important meanings of prayers.

- Prayer is a miss of reporting the enemies to God
- Prayer is a miss of waging war with the enemies.

''*Your trust and hope.*

It will be a wrong identification to believe that our prayer is not much effective and important after either reporting our limits and limitations to God or waiting for answers after we have communicated our challenges to him at the altar of prayer.

Any time that we pray? Heaven is always in attendance in our communication with God. But we need faith in what we are communicating to God, in order for achieving adequate results from God, a dwelling-place.

"*Our trust and hope in God-dwelling place.*

All that differentiates between our responses from the throne of the most-high God! Is how strong we are in the faith.

Remember! Any doubting person can never achieve, any things from God. We all need to have strong faith in our time of the limit and limitations of our lives. Next series! We will be looking into how God responds to our requests or replies to our prayers.

Prayer: the grace to trust and have adequate faith in this season and beyond in the name of Jesus. Amen.

LIVING, BEYOND THE LIMIT! 39

"After understanding all the elements that can make us achieve our uttermost victory over the limit and limitations of our lives?

(Matthew 6:5). And when you pray, do not be like the hypocrites, for they love to pray standing in the synagogues and on the street corners to be seen by others. Truly I tell you, they have received their reward in full.

"It's not the will of God that any of those that are called according to His Holy name is living in the limit and limitations of life.

But there is a divine solving plan that has been divinely put in place for everyone that is called according to the Holy Name of the living lord! To follow in order to live beyond every circumstance or odds that may be befalling them, or what they are experiencing in life. Which is known! As prayer.

The importance of prayer in humans' life? Is beyond human imagination of reasons! Prayers enable and gave everyone that understood the is-importance of a meaningful Christian life.

What happened when we pray and how does God respond to our prayers?

- When we pray, we bring the attention of the whole heaven. And God responds to our prayers either by saying! Yes.

- When we pray, we gave all to God. And God responds to our prayers either by saying! Wait.
- When we pray, we communicate to God. And God responds to our prayers, either by saying! No.

"Knowing when God is saying either Yes, Wait, or No. (Did God Reply) God replied to our prayers in three ways. He could say! Yes, Wait or No. And what are the meanings of these three elements? Yes, Wait and No?

When God says! Yes, to our prayers? It could mean am giving you or it's done. Also, when God says Wait to our prayers? It could mean it's not the right time! Wait it will be given.

And when God says no, to our prayers! It could mean am not giving you. You are asking for the wrong thing.

''Knowing the mind of God, when we pray.

Prayer is a wonderful tool in the lives of every believer in Christ that enables them to have a meaningful Christian life and journey with their faith in Christ.

Also, prayers provide a platform of communication between the believers and their maker! The living Lord. Being a praying believer is all that it takes to understand the mind of God when we pray. Reasons are to the channel of communication between us and God has been well managed and living righteously.

But when one is not a praying believer? To know the mind of God, when either! He is saying Yes, Wait or No! Will not be understood by such one. We need to be praying believers and the limit and limitations of our lives will give way.

Prayer: the grace to be fervent in prayer. In Jesus's name. Amen.

LIVING, BEYOND THE LIMIT! 40

"It's not the will of God that any of those that are called according to His Holy name is living in the limit and limitation of life.

(Matthew 5:8). Blessed are the pure in heart for they shall see God.

"When **carefully looking into the scripture**, how God favoured humans or choose his beloved in his divine purpose on earth, he didn't choose anyone based on stature or how the person looks or what the person has done or managed to achieve in life.

God chooses his beloved and favoured them in his divine purpose on earth, how their heart is a good heart is what enables any human to have a blessed life and achieved one purpose in life and be favoured by God.

An example is David, David in his early life was able to live beyond knowing what he has been destiny for in life and not wondering from not knowing what is ought of him to do in life.

''*A good heart.*

At times is not how fervent we are in prayer and how people around us know some things about our life! That will determine if we are someone with a substantial attitude.

But what will determine it is our inward life. Which can only be discovered and known by God. The state of our inward life! If, is right with God and we are living according to His commandments? No matter the limit and limitations of our life maybe? It will always be defeated and overcome.

''*Overcoming your limit with a right heart.*

A right heart is important in the sight of God! Likewise, having the right heart always makes one live a healthy life and be healthy every day of life.

Also, a right heart qualified one from the multitude and helps one to achieve unachievable dreams and living, beyond every limit and limitation always being won! When one is living with a right heart toward God.

Prayer: your heart will be touched by God in this season in Jesus's name. Amen.

LIVING, BEYOND THE LIMIT! 41

"When carefully looking into the scripture, how God favoured humans or chose his beloved in his divine purpose on earth.

(Acts 2:4). And they were all filled with the Holy Spirit and began to speak with other tongues, as the Spirit gave them utterances.

"**The Holy Spirit is a comforter!** Sent by God. To comfort us in every area of our lives and any time that the limit and limitations may be questioning our faith and trust in the living lord.

The Holy Spirit is a person! That reveals the mind of God to us and shows us the faith in living according to the will and purpose of God for our lives.

Before God, the son ascended to heaven. He promises his disciples that he will not leave them comfortless! That he will send the promise of the father to them, who will show them all things in righteous living and knowing the mind of God for their lives.

Without the presence of the Holy Spirit? Being present in the lives of the disciples of old? The gospel will not have been tremendously achieved or recorded has it had been recorded in the scripture.

''*The comforter*.

As have said that the Holy Spirit is a person sent by God to comfort and show us the mind and the will of God. Also, the Holy Spirit? Being present in our lives! The limit and limitations of life will not gain ground or limit us in progress in the direction of our vision or goal that we might have set to achieve in any space of life.

In other words, as prayer enables any imitators of Christ in achieving success over every limit or limitation of life? Likewise, praying in the spirit! Also, path the way to successful living over every limit that we may be experiencing within life.

"*Praying in the spirit.*

Praying in the heavenly language is also one of the ways of communicating with God! When imitators of Christ pray in the heavenly language? Is the spirit of such imitators of Christ that is communicating with God?

What happens when one prays in the spirit

- There is dynamic communication between imitators and God
- Fresh fire and anointing are being released
- Limits and limitations have no place to hide
- Heavenly intervention
- War in the camp of the enemies and the enemies being defeated .

Prayer: as you will be going to God in praying in the heavenly language! Every limit and limitation that has been questioning your faith in Christ will be defeated in Jesus's name. Amen.

LIVING, BEYOND THE LIMIT! 42

"The Holy Spirit is a comforter, sent by God! To comfort us in every area of our lives.

(Acts 2:17). And it shall come to pass in the last days, says God. That I will pour out my Spirit on all flesh, your sons and your daughters shall prophesy, your young men shall see vision your old men shall dream dreams.

"**To be spiritually healthy and have a substantial relationship with the living Lord** is also adequately important to live beyond every limit and limitation that life may be bringing into one life.

Your spiritual status and how close one is in a relationship with God are very earnestly important if any man will live beyond his or her limit in life.

Believers or an imitator of Christ? That does not have a proper spiritual life! Either, being gifted with the fruit of the spirit and making proper use of the fold of the office of the ministries? Such, believers or an imitator of Christ will ever be longing for how they will achieve a major breakthrough and success in living beyond the limit of life.

"Major breakthrough and success in living beyond the limit of life.

The first principle for anyone that has been longing and wanted to live beyond every mystery that is beyond their capacity of solving? Is by accepting Lord Jesus Christ! Into his or her life.

And in the process of being a family of God? All the gifts that will enable proper achievement in the Christianity journey! Must be substantial achieved by such individuals and having a good relationship with God.

The limit of life does not have the strength to be present or continued with its operation when one is in a full capacity in one Christian life and has a substantial relationship with God.

''*Living to your spiritual capacities.*

When one has gotten an edge over being able to have a full capacity in one spiritual life? The endowment of the Holy Spirit in one life will be in the right direction which God has divinely mandated it to be.

With one gift of the Holy Spirit, being in full capacities and functioning in divine mandate? Limit and limitation will always give way and stop its operation.

Prayer: the grace to be in full capacities and functioning of the Holy Spirit into your life this season and beyond. In Jesus's name. Amen.

LIVING, BEYOND THE LIMIT! 43

"To be spiritually healthy and having a substantial relationship with the living Lord, is also adequately important to live beyond every limit and limitation.

(Romans 1:11). I long to see you so that I may impart to you some spiritual gift to make you strong.

"**Some mysteries that may be beyond one fathom of solving either in spiritual or physical? This** Does not mean such cannot be solved or beyond the solution phenomenon.

Every limit and limitation that has been making life horrible for many, either physical or spiritual? Always has a solving solution that is capable to bring a lasting and ending solution when having the right connection with the right solution plan.

Physical limits and limitations.

Physical limits cannot be solved when utilizing a spiritual mechanism solution plan, to solve and bring an ending and lasting solution. Every circumstance that anyone! May be going through in life? Has are ways of achieving a solution and bringing an ending solution.

In other words, physical limits and limitations can be substantially solved by utilizing physical mechanisms that are surrounded by the physical solving a solution to the physical limits and limitations of life.

''What are the physical limits and limitations of life?

- Joblessness
- Not having adequate academic result
- Lack of sales in business
- Needs and wants are not being adequately achieved
- Not being able to utilize one dream and goals in life
- Financial crises
- Families issues

''*Spiritual limits and limitations.*

As mentioned that to utilize spiritual mechanisms to solve physical limits and limitations? Cannot achieve a lasting ending solution. Likewise, to utilize physical mechanisms to solve spiritual limits and limitations? Also cannot achieve a lasting and ending solution. Every limit and limitation has its own solving mechanism.

What are the spiritual limit and limitations?

- Prayerlessness
- Spiritual crisis
- Not being a lover of Christ
- Not being able to connect to other bodies of Christ
- Lacking the word of God
- Not being able to wait on God for a particular need
- Not being able to fast and pray.

Prayer: every limit and limitation that may be questioning your testimony in Christ! Will give way in your life this season in Jesus's name. Amen.

LIVING, BEYOND THE LIMIT! 44

"Every limit and limitation that has been making life horrible for many, either physical or spiritual? Always has a solving solution.

(Psalm 17:8). Keep me as the apple of your eye; hide me in the shadow of your wings.

"**Talking of protection and to live from all forms of worrisome challenges,** difficulties, and living beyond the limit and limitations of life? Are all lies with God! Not with anyone's abilities or how intelligent one is or how capable one has an edge over any worrisome challenges or difficulties of life.

There are lots of challenges and more things that have been making our faith in God, to be questioning our existences as a believer of Christ, the reasons for their appearances in our lives, and fathoming the imagination of their existences.

God is ever and lasting God! That can protect and give us the victory over any things that we may not have an answer to or the capacity for a lasting solution.

Also, there is no how one can ever live beyond his or her limit when one is far away from God. To be far away from God? Is to be far away from all his protection.

And when one is far away from God? The limit and limitations of one life will always continue with its operation.

''To be far away from God, is to be far away from his protection.

There will always be some form of limit or limitations of life that will want to continue its operation in one endeavour in life, but when the protection of God is missing in one path and ways in life? It will be very difficult to tell the limit and limitations where they belong.

But being in the protection of God? Are what will tell the limit and limitations of our lives to back off from our purpose and destiny.

''Let your limit and limitations back off you.

There is no doubt about achieving our victory in life when we are in the protection of God and daily walking in his purpose for our lives.

Your limit and limitations will always obey the Christ in you! When you are living according to his purpose and being an imitator of Christ.

Prayer: you will not lack the protection of God for your life! In this season and beyond in Jesus's name. Amen.

LIVING, BEYOND THE LIMIT! 45

"Talking of protection and to live from all forms of worrisome, challenges, difficulties, and living beyond the limit and limitations of life? Are all lies with God?

(Psalm 18:2). The LORD is my rock, my fortress, and my deliverer, my God is my rock, in whom I take refuge, my shield and the horn of my salvation, my stronghold.

"**The Lord God** is only the dependable and our assurances when the limit and limitations of our lives are beyond all our strength and effort to handle.

No amount of bits of intelligence anyone maybe or an expert that is well skills in any circumstances that most humans may be experiencing and challenges within life, in helping them out of their limit and limitation? Is little to the strength and availabilities of the sovereignty of God, in giving us lasting and successful living.

Have been able to encounter some mysteries and challenges that most people have confronted and experienced within their lifetime.

Not anyone out of the mysteries that I witness? Could say! Living beyond the limitations lies with their strength and how skills they were.

''*Taking it to God.*

The moment we understood that the only solution to living beyond each of our challenges in life? Cannot be achieved by our bits of intelligence or skills! But can only be achieved when we take it to God. Then we are in line to the lasting solving and successful living in any limit that we may be confronted within our lives.

''*Successful living.*

To be successful is all, that God has in mind for us, it's not the joy of God that any of his beloved are been defeating or been in the circles of limits and limitations of life.

God wants us to prosper and live a healthy life and achieve each of our visions and dreams that we might have set between any space of time and years.

In other words, we can only live in success when we gave all to God and allow him to take us out of all the mysteries that we may be going through in our lifetime.

Prayer; grace to allow God and with his strength to take you out of all your limit and limitations of your life in Jesus's name. Amen.

LIVING, BEYOND THE LIMIT! 46

"The Lord God is only the dependable and our assurances when the limit and limitations of our lives are beyond all our strength and effort to handle.

(Psalm 61:4). I long to dwell in your tent forever and take refuge in the shelter of your wings.

"The psalmist is one of the biblical examples that live beyond his limit and limitations of his life.

He acknowledges the sovereignty and the splendour power of the living Lord that can deliver and bring him out of any mysteries that may be beyond the strength of his abilities to achieve tremendous success and splendour achievement in any mysteries that may be standing between him and his destiny in life.

The psalmist stated that is better for him to dwell in the post door of God Almighty than for him to dwell under the tent of his enemies.

Psalm 84:10 for a day in your court is better than a thousand. I would rather be a doorkeeper in the house of my God than dwell in the tents of wickedness.

In other words, to dwell in the tent of the Almighty God? Is one of the other mechanisms that has been mentioned in this series.

For anyone to allow himself or herself in living under the covering of God? Limits and limitations will always be a stepping achievement toward one projected dreams, goals that have not been yielding to success and achievements.

''Limit and limitations as a stepping achievement in achieving one projected dreams and goals in life.

Continuous and to be diligent in one service and love to God, and to dwell in the shadow of God's winds! Are tremendous achievements over the defeating of one mystery that has been making one projected goals, dreams not to be yielding success in one projected dreams.

"Taking refuge in the shelter of his wings.

The psalmist drew water from the well of knowledge that God is the only source and assurances when the limit and limitations of life are beyond one strength and effort to handle.

Are you in need of achieving a tremendous and lasting victory over your limitations? Then learn how to dwell in the tent of God and to take refuge in the shelter of the winds of the most majesty God.

I will give a few ways to dwell in the shadow of the most majesty God.

- Accepting Lord Jesus Christ as personnel Lord and savour

- Living in righteousness
- Being prayerful
- Daily study of faith and inspirational materials
- Interceding
- Fasting and lastly obedient to tithe and offering.

Prayer: the grace to dwell in the tent and take refuge in the shelter of the wings of God, will be given to you in Jesus's name. Amen.

LIVING, BEYOND THE LIMIT! 47

'The psalmist is one of the biblical examples that live beyond his limit and limitation of his life.

(Psalm 93:1). The Lord reigns, He is clothed with majesty; The Lord is clothed, He has girded Himself with strength. Surely the world is established so that it cannot be moved.

"Forever the living lord will ever be our savour and the one that will give us lasting victory over any limit and limitation that we may be experiencing within our lives.

No matter how subtle and how long the operation of the limitations may be standing between one faith and achievements in one life? To draw water from the well of knowledge as the psalmist did during is limit and limitation of his life! That all power in heaven and on earth belongs to the one that sited in heaven and who make the earth his footstool.

The Almighty God. Is marvellously for our lasting success over our mysteries of the limitation that has been questioning our faith in God.

''*Marvellous success over the limit and limitations.*

The moments we have understood that no how we may have thought or fathomed the reasons of the mysteries of the strange operation of limit and limitations may be!

Either how low or high its operation may be; Nothing in heaven on earth under the earth that will move God to be worry or having not the strength to save us from the odds of imagination of the limit and strange occurrences of our lives.

In other words, he is the king of king and the Lord of Lord, the one that his and his to come. The Almighty God.

''*The Almighty God.*

When limits and limitations throw some challenging experiences into our lives? The Almighty God stops the operation of the odds imagination and stops all forms of thinking and reasoning about where our deliverance will ever come from. The moment we allow our spirit, mind, and soul to rest in the words of God, and what his words are saying to us in regard to the strange circumstances! Then we are in the victory step or being ahead of achieving and living beyond the experiences of the limit and limitations of life.

Prayer: the grace to trust and rest in the word of God in the time of your limit and limitation of your life in Jesus's name. Amen.

LIVING, BEYOND THE LIMIT! 48

"Forever the living Lord will ever be our savour and the one that will give us lasting victory over any limit and limitation that we may be experiencing within life.

(Titus 1:9). Holding fast the faithful word as he has been thought, that he may be able, by sound doctrine, both to exhort and convict those who contradict.

"The in-depth of God's words is also one of the elements or mechanisms of living beyond the limit and limitations of life.

The word of God? Is God itself! That has become flesh which dwells among us. Have more intake of God's words, and be understanding of it! Through the help of the Holy Spirit? Are what that strengthen and enable any believers in Christ to stand firm and be confident in the time of the limit and when the limits have been defeated.

In other words, the operation of limitations or any circumstances at times! It may appear unannounced or uninvited.

But, what will determine when and how the strange odds will be defeated is, what we have inside of us and how obedient's we are to divine instruction.

''*The inside and the obedience.*

Intake of God's words in the lives of believers is like having a light that is never put off. And living to the obedience in the instruction of God's words? Enables any believers to be secure under the shadow wings of the most-high God, and being protected when unannounced or uninvited circumstances may be challenging one faith and strength in the living lord.

"Stop the operation of the limit.

The operation of limits and limitations, being challenging one Christian faith! Is not a healthy experience and is not the will of God for anyone that is diligently in the body of Christ.

The first principle of putting a splendour ending to the operation of the strange odds is when we are able to understand and have full knowledge of who we are in God and what his words are saying about us.

Therefore, when the principle has been well understood, the operations of the strange odds are limited and defeated in our journey to perfection in Christ Jesus.

Prayer: tremendous achievements and a lasting victory in your life! Over the operation of the strange odds circumstances in the name of Jesus. Amen.

LIVING, BEYOND THE LIMIT! 49

'The in-depth of God words, is also one of the elements or mechanism of living beyond the limit and limitations of life.

(Philemon's 1:4). Hearing of your love and faith, which you have toward the Lord Jesus and toward all the saints.

"**Giving oneself continuously to the work of God**, either in winning souls to the kingdom of God or be making one available in the services of God in one place of one worship and being trusted to the kingdom business is the landmark of achieving substantial and tremendous result over the limit and limitations of life.

When one has been fully involved in the kingdom business and living to all the instruction that has been given by God? Such individuals have been identified as blessed believers of Christ.

And when heaven has identified one has blessed believers? No limit and limitations of life can have held such one in the strange mysteries and circumstances.

In other words, continuous involvement in the kingdom business is what enables one to have a divine edge and defeat every operation of limits and limitations of life.

''*Your kingdom business defeating the operations of the limits.*

As mentioned in the previous series that folding of arms and doing nothing with regard to the operations of odds circumstances activities of strange mysteries will not help or bring lasting solutions! But it will only add more of its operations in one life, Meanwhile, diligences of one kingdom business or daily Christian walk of faith in God, are what will strengthen and give one victory over the limitation of life.

''*When the limit and limitation of life is confronting.*

There will always be some form of challenges or strange mysteries that will want to challenge one faith and Christian walk in Christ which one didn't expect such mysteries to be confronting one at any particular time or season.

But the seed that one has sown in the kingdom business or one daily walk of faith that will enable one to stand and coming out strongly and victoriously in the strange mysteries.

Prayer: the oil and grace to be involved in the kingdom business and daily walk in faith in Christ Jesus into your life! This season and beyond. In Jesus's name. Amen.

LIVING, BEYOND THE LIMIT! 50

"Giving oneself continuously to the work of God, either in winning souls to the kingdom of God or by making one available in the services of God in one place of one worship.

(Philemon 1:6). That the sharing of your faith may become effective by the acknowledgement of every good thing which is in you in Christ Jesus.

"**Testifying of the goodness of God among believers and appreciating the loving-kindness and his marvellous blessings in our life!** Paths-the-way of glorious achievements and winning the substantial battle over the limit and limitation of life that has been standing in one path of living successfully in life.

Every success achieved or any successful people that we may discover or living in the atmosphere of great achievers in our surrounding or world? Always have the roots of the sources of their success and how their success has been achieved.

In other words, success achieves in righteousness and that has its root in Christ. Are what keep one destiny and purpose that has been divine to materialize and affect humanity positively, and keeping such purpose and destiny from the substantial parameter distances from any limit and limitation of life.

''*Success achieved outside righteousness.*

As success is achieved in righteousness keeping one dream goals from substantial parameter distances of the limit and limitations of life? Whereas, success achieves outside righteousness! Continuously making one a slave to the limit and limitations of life.

Due to the root of how the success has been achieved! One cannot come out boldly and wage war with any form of limit and the strange odds, that life may be throwing at one if such success has been rooted in darkness.

''*Coming out boldly over your odds challenging.*

When biblical understood that to win a glorious success in waging war with strange occurrences and challenges of life, lies in having a relationship with the living Lord and living to all the instruction mandate that he has mandated for every believer and those that diligently seek him in truth and honesty.

Then such one can confront the limit and limitations of life with the name of the Lord and by their word of testimony.

Prayer: your testimony of the doing of God in your life will keep you from substantial parameters distances over

every limit and limitation of life.
In Jesus's name. Amen.

LIVING, BEYOND THE LIMIT! 51

''Testifying of the goodness of God among believers and appreciating the loving-kindness and his marvellous blessings in our life! Paths the way to glorious achievements.

(Revelation 1:8). I am the Alpha and the Omega, the beginning and the End, ''Says the Lord. 'Who is and who was and is to come the Almighty.

''**Acknowledgement of the sovereignty of the glorious God and who he is to us,** giving us the courage and the strength to live in the acknowledgement that, no matter how strange occurrences may continue operating and challenging our stand in the belief that God Almighty is not able and mighty to bring us out of the strange occurrence.

Yielding to the subtle, the tone, and the ideology of its manifestation in one life? Will make one live in slaves of the limit and limitations and taking one from the promises and the grace of God, for overcoming every operation of strange mysteries and the limit that may be challenging one believes in God.

In other words, before we foresee any strange manifestation of the strange mysteries that have been throwing all forms of mysteries for us to imagine is existences? God Almighty has remained the beginning and the ending.

''The Alpha and the omega.

As God is the God of the beginning and the ending? No strange occurrences that we may be experiencing or the limit that has been hindering one life not to achieve, or experiencing greatness! It's bigger than God, high than God, or has been in existence from the beginning?

Nothing that's in existence in this world both in heaven and on earth under the earth that is created or formed by itself.

Everything that has been discovered in the human world! Are all created by God, the Alpha and the omega.

''Are the strange odds from God.

God is the God of light and righteousness in him, there is no darkness.

As have said that he created everything both in heaven, on earth under the earth! He knows our challenges and every limit and limitation that we may be experiencing. Even before they started their odds operations in our life.

Glory to his Holy name! For the joy of salvation and our faith in him, which enables us to stand strong and walk tall in the miss of odds occurrences. And by our acknowledgement of who he is to us? The operation of limit has no ground and hold to continue or put us to slavering. By our acknowledgement of God, the limit and limitations will continue to be defeated.

Prayer: the grace to acknowledge the sovereignty and the glorious God into your

life today and beyond in Jesus's name. Amen.

LIVING, BEYOND THE LIMIT! 52

"Acknowledgement of the sovereignty of the glorious God and who he is to us, giving us the courage and the strength.

(Jude 1:2). Mercy, peace, and love be multiplied to you.

"**The reasons,** purpose, and the diligence of the reasons with the foundation of a man in Christ and in one endeavour? Also is the element of achieving substantial results over any unannounced limit and limitations of life.

Without one living an adequate meaningful life, that one has been able to establish a meaningful foundation from his or her onset towards the immediate and the future! When unannounced circumstances try to influence or take advantage of such a life? Will only turn into a wind that blows in and out.

Due to such life, has already been adequately seasoned with a substantial foundation in their purpose-driving goal. In other words, any life that does not well seasoning either from the onset of setting out its purpose or having a meaningful foundation? When unannounced forces attacked such life will only be a target of such unannounced circumstances.

''Limits and limitations as the wind blow in and out.

What it takes to have authority in any space of life, season and time! Is when one foundation has been well established and managed. The Bible does mention the righteous and its foundation.

Psalm 11:3 if the foundations are destroyed what can the righteous do?

The foundation needs to be managed in order to lay a rightful purpose and to be diligent in pursuing the purpose-driving goal.

Meanwhile, the reasons, purpose, and diligently towards the purpose-driving goal? Are all strengthening when the foundation has been well established?

"Mercy, peace, and love be multiplied to you.

No, how unannounced the limit of life may seem and all are strategies, when one has been adequately established from the onset of any area of purpose and adequately pursuing it in righteousness, in what has been well established in a splendours foundation.

The mercy and peace of God will be multiplying in one life, even when any strange mysteries blow in or occurred in any process of achieving one purpose in life, and by good establishments of substantial foundation, purpose, and diligence towards the purpose-driving goal! The way the limit and limitation blow in shall they blow out.

Prayer: your foundation will be meaningful and seasoned with favour in Christ in your immediate and in the future. In Jesus's name. Amen.

"Living beyond the limit"...

BOOKS WRITTEN BY SHALOM:

Getting a Big break

Why Black Why Not White

Lord you are my deliverer

More of you lord

Living beyond the limit

Secret of an Imitator

Vision and you

You will know

Reasons

Great success

The Secret of an Achiever

Dominion: Sermon

The key of Success: Sermon

Hour of Solution with Jesus: Sermon

BOOKS WRITTEN BY SHALOM:

Filter and taking away the chaff

Excellent God

The peculiar

The children of Zebedee's

Free from the trapped

He call

You will know

Living beyond the limit: program module vol one.

In God not In God

Living beyond the limit: program module vol two.

Shalom is the director of; Adebisi Dawodu SA, ministries that based in Rooihuiskraal Centurion. And the C.E.O of Adebisi Shalom Trading Enterprises

South Africa.

For prayers and counseling?

Send your request to: aslileadership@gmail.com

Website site: aste-sa.business.site

Independently published (July 23, 2018)

Republic of South Africa

Living beyond the limit

www.ingramcontent.com/pod-product-compliance
Lightning Source LLC
Chambersburg PA
CBHW051821090426
42736CB00011B/1582
9780994705549